Dick,

Follow your Dreams...

Dream Bigger!

If your website was an employee, would you fire it?

5 things you wish you knew
before you made your website
...and how to fix them now

marketing & publishing

IF YOUR WEBSITE WAS AN EMPLOYEE, WOULD YOU FIRE IT?

ISBN 9780983211907
LCCN 2010919220

Published by
Left of Center Marketing & Publishing
Kendall Park, NJ

Acknowledgements:
I would like to thank the following for their contributions to this book
Editor: Jamie Gough
Book Design: Thomas Kato
Cover Design: Ian Berg

While I have already dedicated my life to her,

I want to also dedicate this book

to my wife, Carole. You are my conscience,

my sounding board and my inspiration.

TABLE OF CONTENTS

INTRODUCTION

Thanks for picking up my book. There's no shortage of things competing for your attention, so before we get started, I want to thank you for spending this time with me.

As a professional speaker, I choose my topics for the audiences that are kind enough to make the time to listen to me. To respect my audiences I ask myself, who are they? What are their goals? What value can I bring to them that will help them achieve their goals? The subject of this book started as a presentation I gave to a varied group of wedding professionals at a conference in Las Vegas. The event producer asked me to prepare an entirely new presentation that would benefit everyone—or at least mostly everyone— who would be attending. As I thought about who my audience would be, what their goals were and what I could bring to them, it occurred to me that they should be asking some of the same questions of themselves in regard to their marketing, and more specifically, their websites. I knew they would be an audience composed mostly of small business owners whose main services and products were geared towards brides. Through my more than 20 years of dealing with businesses like theirs, and through having owned my own small businesses, I was pretty sure that most of them hadn't approached their website design in a rational, well-planned manner.

I've been giving presentations to small businesses about sales and marketing topics for around 15 years, and while I still love to speak about print, direct mail and email marketing, the last few years have brought me more and more opportunities to talk about websites and social media. I would have to say that the turning point at which I began to focus more fully on websites was in 2006, while I was vice president of local sales at The Knot (the leading lifestage media company providing wedding planning tips to engaged couples through the Internet, magazines and other media). One of our account executives called me to say that a local videography advertiser had requested to cancel his ad on TheKnot.com (the largest, busiest, wedding media site). Despite having advertised with us for over 10 years, and having the second-highest tracking ratings for page views and click-throughs in his market and category, this videographer was convinced that his ad with us wasn't working.

The tracking clearly showed that we were getting hundreds of brides to look at his ad and click through to his site, which told me that his ad was working. So, I followed the trail and looked at his website to see what the brides were seeing. I couldn't believe what I found. This was a wedding videographer, yet there wasn't one photo of a bride—his target audience— anywhere on his site. Oh, there were photos... of him wearing a tuxedo in his office (which is in his house—I'm sure he dresses this way every day). In addition, there was a photo of his wife (and business partner), also in a tuxedo, sitting at her desk, in their house. In the photos, I could see an editing console and a video demo viewing room, with a relatively small television and a dated, flowery sofa to boot.

I was floored. How could any bride be expected to feel as though she had arrived at a professional wedding videographer's site? The navigation was poor, the site looked outdated and worst of all, my first thought was that he must have made the site himself. Now, don't get me wrong. If you happen to be an expert at whatever your service or product is and you also happen to be a professional website designer, then go ahead and make it yourself. It just shouldn't look like you did.

After I got up off the floor, I wrote a multi-page e-mail to the videographer detailing, website page by website page, how to address the weaknesses of his site so he could see better results: not just from his ads with The Knot, but from all sources of traffic. Good news:

The customer didn't cancel. Bad news: The customer didn't change anything on his site for over a year. And when he did, he hardly addressed any of the things I had suggested.

But something good did come of this encounter: After having sent the videographer my e-mail , I sat down and started typing a new presentation: "10 Ways Your Website May Be Costing You Money". For many months, I offered this presentation to various groups and events, with no takers.

Then one event producer invited me to speak at his conference for wedding professionals and I told him that I would do it only if I could present about this particular topic. In fact, he even tweaked the title to "10 Ways Your Website Is Killing Your Business," and it certainly is catchier. The presentation that is the basis of this book, "5 things you wish you'd known before you made your website", is either the prequel or the sequel to that presentation, depending upon how you look at it.

So, I want thank the videography advertiser (who will remain anonymous), the account executive at The Knot and the event producer for helping me put together these critical points about website design. I also want to thank all of the wonderful business owners who I've had the privilege to meet through my live presentations and webinars, and through my 20-plus years in sales, advertising and marketing. We're all a product of our experiences—and that makes you a part of mine.

My goal for this book is to help you see what your website can and should be. These ideas work for almost any website, regardless of what business you're in, no matter what you're offering your visitors. They're just as applicable to an auto mechanic as a wedding photographer. They'll help a doctor improve her website just as they'll help a reception site. Most of the examples in this book will refer to wedding professionals as most of the businesses that I work with are seeking out brides. I know that you'l be able to read between the lines and see how to apply these to your business, no matter what you do.

Most of these ideas will cost you little or nothing to implement. I want you to discover your site's full potential, and see that it won't take boatloads of cash to get there. So are you ready? Let's get you started on your way to a great website.

CHAPTER ONE

Moving in the Right Direction:
Whether You're Improving Your Site
or Starting a New One

Do You Have to Start Over?

You've made an important first step by picking up this book. You're acknowledging that your web presence potentially needs improving. For many businesses, a website is one of the first—if not the first—contact they'll have with potential clients... so it's extremely important. Adding fresh content can get former visitors to return, and it's also one of the foundations of good search engine optimization (SEO), which helps drive new visitors to your site. Will you need to start over from scratch, or simply improve your existing website? By the end of this short book, you'll be in a better position to decide which approach is right for you. If you do decide to start over, you'll learn some easy things that you can do to spruce up your current website while you work on that new one.

IF YOUR WEBSITE WAS AN EMPLOYEE, WOULD YOU FIRE IT?: *Five Things You Wish You Knew Before You Made Your Website (and a few more if you're really counting)* will help you give your site's visitors an informative, interactive and interesting experience. The five things are actually five questions that you should be asking yourself—whether your planning a new site, or hoping to improve the one you've already got. The questions will sound simple, but the answers will require some thought and introspection on your part. The good news is that you already know the answers: Just be honest with yourself about the types of clients you have and your business goals, and you'll get the best results from this book.

Oh, and don't worry: This is not one of those books that makes you do a lot of homework to get results. In my experience, while the concepts in such books are interesting, most people I know, myself included, rarely follow through if the homework is too involved. It's not that we don't see the value in it, it's that everyday life and business just get in the way.

> **NOTE:** Approach Your Website Design Like It's a Conversation Between You and Your Site Visitors

I've had a very successful career as a professional sales person. Most people who know me wouldn't believe that I was a relatively shy child, at least in new situations. Now my wife contends that she could drop me in almost any new situation and I'd come out with some new friends. One of the skills that I've learned, and honed, over the years, is that asking better questions yields better results for both parties: those who are seeking information, and those who are providing it. That's true in social situations and in business.

Imagine meeting someone for the first time and asking them, *"What do you do?"* to which they proceed to drone on and on and on, for 10 minutes straight, seemingly without coming up for air. You wouldn't feel very good about the encounter because it would clearly show the speaker's lack of interest in you.

Now, let's say they give a short answer, then ask, *"And what do you do?",* and then they stop talking and actually listen intently to your answer. After your reply, they ask, *"How did you happen to choose that field?"* This back and forth goes on for a while.

Which conversation makes you feel better? The first shows that they're only interested in telling you about themselves. The second one engages you and shows that the other person is interested in hearing about you. Most websites that I see for smaller businesses tend to be like the first conversation, if you can even call it a conversation. Those websites are a continuous drone about those businesses, from the standpoint of those businesses. The sites don't take into consideration who's visiting or what their needs and goals are. The result is basically a bad resume or brochure for those businesses and their owners.

Read on to find out how you can improve your site and make it into a truly engaging conversation with your prospects.

CHAPTER TWO

Question One:
Who Is Your Site's Audience

Sounds simple, doesn't it? Who's going to be visiting your site? You know that answer, or do you? Let's say you're a florist and you provide arrangements for weddings, funerals, bar mitzvahs, everyday and holidays. Now, who's the audience for your website? Not such a short answer, is it?

Let's make it easier. You're a wedding floral designer. You don't provide flowers for any other events or occasions. Now, who's the audience for your website? You're probably thinking, *It's brides.* But is it ALL brides? Probably not.

Narrowing Down Who Your Audience Is

First of all, it's the brides who live in or are getting married in your trading area, not all brides in the United States. That's easy. Next, is it brides of all budgets? Again, probably not. What about your style: Does it appeal to all brides in your market? Again, probably not. Even if you have a wide range of services, you're not going to be the right floral designer for all brides in your market. The brides that walk into the town hall for a civil ceremony, carrying a small bouquet of flowers, are probably not your prospects. Assuming they don't buy the flowers from a vending machine at the courthouse, they'll probably buy them from a full service retail florist.

No matter what business you're in you need to determine if you have one definable audience or many potential audiences. You also need to be as specific and honest with yourself as possible. Who are they? What criteria can you use to define them? Can you use age, income, zip code, education, ethnicity and/ or style? This specificity will not only help you design your site or sites, but it'll also help you focus your marketing on the prospects who are most likely to use your products and services.

Defining Personas

A persona is a detailed description of the typical client from a particular audience that works with your business. I remember reading a case study about how BestBuy divided the contents of its stores into sections for five distinct personas. It defined each of these five personas as clearly as it could by demographics (including age, sex, income and marital status) and psychographics (the way these customers think and approach purchasing items like those sold at BestBuy).

Defining these personas helped BestBuy determine how to organize its stores, which merchandise to make available and how the sales team should interact with the customers who seemed to fit these personas. For example, the needs of a single man in his early thirties who's looking for a high-end television are very different from the needs of a married woman in her thirties, with two small children in tow, who's looking for a major appliance. The motivations of these customers are clearly varied. The way BestBuy's sales representatives talk to them and which product features they promote are different, and are driven by BestBuy's development of those personas.

Your Clients' Personas

Can you create the persona of your typical or ideal customers? We already determined that if you're a florist looking for brides, that doesn't include ALL brides, so can you put that description of your ideal bridal customer into words?

Here's an idea of how this persona description might look for our florist example: This persona is a single woman, currently engaged, college educated with a wedding date 6 to 14 months in the future. She has a household income of $50,000 to $85,000, considers herself a trendsetter, likes a contemporary style with a nod toward classic touches and lives within 35 miles of your business location. And, of course, she hasn't yet booked someone for her wedding flowers.

Now, let's imagine that you're a photographer who's looking for corporate work. You would define the corporation that you're looking for by considering which industries that customer might work in, what type of products/services they might provide, the size of their company, the location of their company, what kinds of photography they use, the decision maker's role in the company, etc.

The more specific you can be about the persona, the better. If you specialize in doing business with a certain religious or ethnic group, add that to the description of the persona. If you cater to a niche market such as those having a destination wedding, or the gay or second marriage market, add that as well. All of these definitions will not only help you understand your market better, they'll also help you most effectively advertise to them. Since advertising is about "buying" access to an audience, knowing more clearly which audience you're actually looking for helps you find and target them better.

Your business can, and likely will have more than one audience (and therefore, more than one persona). If you have very distinct lines of business, this is a very useful exercise to help you identify each persona of your business and the marketing that'll be most effective for each of those different personas. Unless the entire population is your market, you should be advertising to each persona separately. It's much more efficient to be laser focused on each type of customer instead of using the shotgun approach and sending your message to everyone with the hopes of getting some of the right clients to find you. It's not likely that you have the kind of budget needed for large-scale marketing, so defining your business's personas is a great first step.

Remember to Be Honest with Yourself

Define only the customers you're targeting right now. If you want to change who you market to—whether you're adding an additional line of business or moving your current business in a new direction (e.g., focusing on more upscale clients or changing your business model altogether)—first make the necessary changes to your business, then figure out how to market to that audience. If you make the marketing changes first, when clients from that new audience speak to or meet with you, they'll discover that your business is not yet the business you're trying presenting yourself to be, and you won't make the sale.

For example, if you're a reception site for weddings and other events, and you want to move your business up to a more elegant, upscale audience, you must first make the changes to your physical location (by upgrading your decor, dishes, restrooms, etc.), next upgrade your menu and products, then you can market your business as an upscale reception site.

If you don't make the upgrades to your building and menus, then the prospective brides who are attracted by your new upscale marketing will show up for their appointments, see that your physical location doesn't look upscale, and they'll leave. Similarly, if you're trying to attract corporate meeting business, but you haven't yet invested in the technology required for meeting facilities, your target audience may be attracted by your marketing, but won't be willing to book your venue until you show that you're ready, and able, to fulfill their meeting needs. Your marketing has to match everything you offer them. That's why a Mercedes Benz dealership looks and feels different than a Hyundai dealership: Each dealership visually represents the price and class of the cars being sold there and the customers who buy them.

A Note About Advertising

I've often said that one of the basic tenets of advertising is knowing who your target audience is and then putting yourself in front of as many of them as you can. When you invest in advertising, you're not buying an ad, you're buying access to that media's audience, and using the ads to attract them to you. So getting your ads in front of the right audience—the one most likely to have interest in your products and services— is a very important aspect of good marketing. First locate the right audience, then decide which type of ad to invest in.

CHAPTER THREE

Do You Need Additional Sites or Landing Pages?

If you've determined that you have more than one target audience, these questions naturally follow:

1) Should you have one website with separate areas for each audience?

You can have one big website with distinct areas for each type of potential client who visits your site. If your audiences are likely to need the other products or services that you provide, having one website will help them with their current needs while informing them of your other services. Make sure that your site's navigation is straight-forward and easy to follow so each audience can find what they need.

2) Should you have separate websites for each audience?

If your audiences are very different, or at least at the time they first find your website their needs are very different (for example, people visiting your site for weddings have very different needs than those visiting for funerals - don't laugh, this is a real example from a dove-release business I met), then having completely separate websites is a good way to show each audience that you understand their needs and have the professional skills to satisfy them. On each website, you can have subtle links to your other sites while keeping your message very focused on the current audience's particular needs. This approach minimizes the distractions for your site visitors and lets you present yourself as a specialist for their current need—as opposed to a generalist or jack-of-all-trades.

3) Should you use separate landing pages for each audience?

A landing page is the first page that a particular visitor to your website sees (i.e., where they "land" on your site). If you have a landing page, they'll usually see it before arriving at your website's home page. You can have many different landing pages: one for each of the audiences for your business. Landing pages are extremely helpful when you have one, large website for very different audiences. They can help each visitor find the content that's most relevant to them without having to search for it. You can think of landing pages as home pages for each audience.

Let's say you're a videographer, and that you advertise your services on the wedding planning site, WeddingChannel.com. You know that anyone who clicks on your ad from WeddingChannel.com is likely to be a bride who's looking for a wedding videographer. You could develop a landing page where that ad would immediately lead, so that after clicking your ad, the next

IF YOUR WEBSITE WAS AN EMPLOYEE, WOULD YOU FIRE IT?

page that person would see would acknowledge that: **1)** You know this person came from WeddingChannel. com; **2)** You know they're interested in wedding information (as opposed to corporate or other services you offer); and **3)** You know they've seen and read at least a little about your business on the ad from which they clicked.

To design a landing page for this scenario, you'd think of everything such a visitor would want to see and do on your site, and then provide clearly labeled links to the areas that provide that information. For example, they'd likely want to see videos of weddings and information about your wedding packages, so your landing page would include links titled, "Video Gallery" and "Wedding Packages," which would lead directly to those areas on your website as well as a few others.

Landing Page for Wedding Photography

Now, let's imagine that you're a wedding photographer. We'll make a list of things a bride might want to do after clicking your online ad at TheKnot.com. That list could include, 1) Seeing more photo galleries (since your ad has a gallery of images), 2) Checking on your availability for her wedding date, 3) Scheduling an appointment, 4) Seeing your prices, and 5) Reading testimonials.

Your landing page can start by welcoming her to your site, thanking her for coming, then asking her, "How can I help you today?" followed by a few beautiful pictures of brides, and clearly named links to the things you just determined she's likely to want, including a link to your home page. Make sure your landing page, as with every page on your site, also includes a clear call to action with your contact information. An example of a relevant call to action on this page would be "*For more information, or to arrange an appointment with our wedding specialists, call or email today, 800-555-1212*".

At this point, you've provided the prospective bride with a limited number of choices, but they're the most likely choices she'll need, so you've given her a very helpful introduction to your services and made it easy for her to take action.

Landing Page for Corporate Photography

Let's say that as a photographer, you also do corporate work. Brides and corporations are different demographics, with different needs, and therefore their landing pages should have different designs and links. Your approach, however, is very much the same. You're still going to thank them for coming and ask, "How can we help you today?", but the links you provide to additional information on your site won't be the same. The images you show on this landing page will also be different than the one for weddings: Instead of showing brides, you'll show samples of your corporate work. You'll use language showing corporate visitors that you understand corporate needs and that you're the right professional who can fulfill those needs. The images and text are different but the concept is the same.

CHAPTER FOUR

Give Your Site Visitors Something to Aspire To

Advertising Is Aspirational

Most advertising is aspirational: It makes us aspire to be like the people we see in the ads who are using a particular product or brand. That's why most of the ads you see or hear—whether on television, on radio, in print, online or on billboards—have people in them. The intent of the advertisers is that the people you see and hear are doing things you'd want to see yourself doing: driving a nice car, wearing nice clothing, eating great food and so on. Their goal is make us want to be like the people in their ads.

When my two sons were small, my wife and I always had minivans. They were the perfect vehicle for getting around locally and long distance with our kids. We had room for our children and the many, many things that accompanied them: strollers, bikes, toys and more. When I see the ads for minivans now, with the dual DVD players, seats that fold into the floor (instead of having to be removed as ours did) and lots of storage compartments, I can imagine other parents wishing that they were the people in the ads, whose lives look calm and organized, and whose kids were sitting quietly in the car.

Ads Show Us Who We Want to Be

It's no surprise that brides love magazines. The Knot national wedding magazine typically contains over 800 photos of wedding dresses. Virtually all of those images are of very tall, very thin women who are size 0 or 2. When I speak to the bridal gown retailers around the country, they tell me that the typical sample sizes in their stores are 8, 10 or 12. That size discrepancy is a pretty big disconnect between what's in the ad and what the average bride is wearing.

However, what the advertisers are counting on is that the women seeing the ad are going to use their mental "erasers" and replace the face of that size 2 model with their own, while thinking, *"If I wear that dress, that's what I'll look like at my wedding."* **In other words, they'll aspire to be like the woman in the ad.** This is the basis for all fashion advertising. You rarely see the clothing without people wearing it. It's really the basis for almost all advertising, regardless of what's being sold: cola, cars, sunglasses, even water.

Show Your Potential Clients What They Can Aspire To

What do you want your potential customers to feel when they interact with your ads? You want them to associate with the people in your ads, and to desire to be just like them.

Remember the persona I talked about earlier in this book? Ask yourself who represents your prototypical customer. What image can you use that will make your prospects want to replace the images of the people in your ad with their own?

It amazes me to see ads for wedding reception venues that are trying to attract brides yet they only show photos of empty banquet rooms, empty gardens and empty gazebos. Where are the people? A photo of a beautiful view from the balcony of your venue is a nice photo, but it doesn't scream, *"Wedding!"* Show a bride, or—even better—a bride and groom taking in that beautiful view, and the photo of your venue changes immediately to the photo of a wedding location.

You can apply this same principle to most businesses: **Don't just show your product; show people interacting with your product, and make sure they look the way the people you're trying to attract want to see themselves.**

Applying the Concept to Service-Based Businesses

What if your business is a service, such as a wedding planner or disk jockey? How do you show your clients something to aspire towards? You can show the *results* of your work.

Wedding planners help brides with the details of their weddings, so show a happy bride with her bouquet or at the ceremony. You can show detail shots of the decorations in your photo galleries after she sees some people.

Disk jockeys set the tone for the party, so show a smiling bride and groom dancing with their guests. If you can get a shot of them dancing that has you, in action, in the background, that's even better, and it'll show off how professionally you present yourself at an event such as theirs.

Applying the Concept to Product-Based Businesses

What about people who sell products, such as invitations or favors (yes—pretty much all of my examples are based on weddings: they're what I know best but you can apply this concept to whatever you do)? Again, show your prospects what they aspire towards: pictures of pleased looking guests opening elegantly designed invitations, or smiling guests enjoying their fun wedding favors. A neat way to tie in product shots with your target audience is to show a photo of the product, let's say an invitation, and then show a photo of that bride whose wedding it was from. It not only adds a face to the product, it shows that it's from a real wedding and not just a demo.

Note for Product-Based Businesses

Of course, the medium on which your prospect is viewing your photos also makes a big difference (brochure, website, print ad, postcard, etc.). The one constant is that the images have to be high quality and professional looking. If you own a product-based business and you need to show close-up details for one of your products, offer a way for viewers to zoom in, or else use an inset shot with a close up of the important details. If there's some aspect of a product that makes it unique, but that isn't immediately visible in a photo, show your potential client where to look for it. Don't be subtle here: Tell them exactly what it is that makes your product unique. It will also help your SEO to have as much descriptive text as possible on your site.

Should You Show Yourself in Your Ads?

Now, I can hear some of you saying, *"Alan, I want to show a picture of myself since it's me they're hiring."* Of course they're hiring you, but unless you're a legitimate celebrity, with universal recognition (and not just a celebrity in your own mind), your target audience likely includes many people who don't know you yet. Using a photo of yourself will not attract as many prospects as if you showed a more engaging, aspirational image. They don't want to aspire to be like you, they want to aspire to be like people they can relate to, using your services.

I suggest starting with an aspirational image on your home page or landing page, and then you can use a photo gallery elsewhere on your site, and include images of you and your team. Your "About Us" page on your website is a perfect place for that too. A nice touch would be a photo of you with a real, smiling bride, or whoever your customer is. It sends the message that she was so happy working with you that she wanted to have her picture taken with you on her wedding day.

CHAPTER FIVE

Question 2: How Will People Get to Your Website?

This too sounds like an easy question, but is it? There are many, many ways that someone can arrive at your website. Here are a few:

» By clicking on an ad you've placed online

» By finding and clicking on your listing in a search engine (i.e., unpaid placement through SEO)

» By seeing and clicking on your search engine marketing ads (keyword ads you've paid to have placed on search engines)

» By typing in your website's address from a print ad

» By typing in your website's address from your collateral material: brochures, business cards, mailing pieces, etc.

» By clicking on a link in an email that you sent her, or one that was sent for you (a paid email advertisement)

» By clicking on your link from another website, perhaps the website of someone in your industry with whom you've traded links

» By clicking on your link from your blog (if it's not directly a part of your website, which it should be)

» By clicking on your link from someone else's blog (perhaps the blog of someone who referenced you because they've used your services, or who works in your industry)

» By clicking on your link from a social media site (e.g., Facebook, MySpace or LinkedIn)

» By clicking on a link from your photo or video content on a site like YouTube, Vimeo or Flickr

Consider What Prospects Know About Your Business When They Arrive at Your Site

What I want you to think about here is what each of these visitors knows about your business when they arrive at your site. Someone coming from an online ad or a print ad in a magazine already knows something about your company (what they saw and read in the ad), while someone coming from a search engine may know very little about it. Someone who clicked your link that's provided on another website may only know that you were on the list of recommended "Invitation Designers," but they don't know what types of invitations you create, your price range, location or your personality. When these prospects arrive at your site, they'll need to have more information than someone who came from your online ad who already has an idea of the types of invitations you design. Again, this is where landing pages can be useful in taking each audience from each separate entry path to the next logical step, rather than moving them back a step, or more, to your home page.

Choosing the Right Medium for Your Ads

Good advertising acts like a filter. It filters everyone who sees your ad down to those who are most interested in your product or service.

Choosing the right medium for your ads is part of the filtering process. If you're looking for brides, you wouldn't advertise in a men's sports magazine. Even placing the most well designed wedding ad in that men's sports magazine would be unlikely to yield significant results. When you choose a magazine or website in which to advertise, and you buy your placement based upon the size and quality of the audience who uses that medium, you're using a filter so that only the most promising prospects will see your ads. All media filters a larger audience down to a more targeted one. Then, your ad on that media *itself* acts as a finer filter by attracting the right prospects from the already filtered audience: those who *need, want* and *can afford* your service.

All clicks are not created equal

When considering which media to use for ads, you must factor in the conversion rate for those media. The conversion rate is the number of prospects (i.e., people who see your ad) who contact you and then become customers. You don't just want more people viewing your ads: you want more of the right people— those who want your type of service or product—to view them. For online ads, for example, I have people telling me all the time that they buy their ads based upon the cost per click to their website link. But your cost per click is irrelevant if you don't know how much business you're getting from each click. When I ask those same people what their revenue per click is (how much money they average from each click to their website from an online ad), the room goes silent. They don't know, because they fail to connect the dots from the ad to the actual business it creates.

Advertising is not about the costs; it's about the *return on your investment* (ROI). If you can get a positive ROI from a particular advertising method, then you should probably do it.

Let's say you're a professional videographer and your average job brings you $3,000. Does it really matter if the average cost per click of an ad is $1, $5, or $50 if every one of those clicks brings you an average of $3,000? Of course not. Now, let's say that one of the websites on which you advertise brings you three times as many clicks as another site, but no more revenue. Your cost per click may be lower, but your bottom line is no richer. So you see, cost per click is not enough information: You need to follow the trail all the way to the sale.

I could write a whole book on conversion and ROI...

Hey, that's not a bad idea... stay tuned.

CHAPTER SIX

Tracking Your Website Traffic to Learn Your Visitors' Needs

Nowadays, there are many free resources for "tracking" your website traffic. For example, Google Analytics tells you the number of visitors to your site, where they came from (i.e., did they click a particular ad, your profile on Facebook, or did they click your link on a friend's site?) and even which was the last page they viewed before exiting your site. Website tracking software provides invaluable insight into how your visitors are interacting with your site. If you aren't currently tracking your site's traffic, I would advise you to start as soon as possible.

One caveat about tracking software: don't just install the tracking software, you need to also learn how to read the reports. If you don't know how to interpret the data you'll end up making important business decisions based upon incomplete, or wrong, information.

Consider Hiring a Web Master

Your webmaster can help you with reading your tracking reports and setting up tracking if you don't have it already. Don't have a webmaster? This is yet another reason to hire a professional to make your site. You want your prospects to hire you because you're a professional in your industry. Shouldn't you use the same logic when it comes to your website... which is likely to be your prospect's first impression of your business?

Follow the Bouncing Visitor

One way to gauge the quality of the visitors to your website from different sources is by looking at your *bounce rate.*

What's a *bounce rate?* Have you ever clicked onto a website, only to find that it wasn't what you were looking for, so you left without visiting any other pages on that site? You left from the same page on which you arrived, so you *bounced* off that site.

On your site's tracking report, look at the bounce rate from each traffic source (i.e., referring site, search term or ad) and type of traffic. The lower the bounce rate for a particular source, the more relevant your site was to them and therefore the more likely it is that visitors from that source will become clients. This still doesn't tell you if those site visitors actually go on to do business with you, but if they leave from the same page on which they enter, you have no shot of getting their business. They're gone.

I had a customer tell me that Facebook was their top source for incoming traffic, but when I looked at their Google Analytics report, those Facebook clicks had a 78-percent bounce rate. That means that only 22 percent of the people who came in from Facebook were sticking around to see more than that one page. According to their analytics, other sources of traffic to the site resulted in fewer total visits, but had much lower bounce rates. For this business Facebook was bringing quantity, but not quality traffic. In addition, this customer wasn't tracking the conversion rates of different media where they advertised. In other words they knew where their traffic was coming from, but they didn't know if those visitors were becoming customers. They could have done this by asking each client how they'd gotten to their website (while they were still on it), where they found their email or where they got their phone number (when they first call). Then they could connect the dots between the website traffic and the sales those visits generated.

Identifying Trends in Your Site Visitors

Website tracking software is great for spotting trends in your traffic and for seeing which pages get visited the most. One thing you can do is look to see which pages on your site people are coming from to get to your online contact form. Then you'll see which pages have the best conversion rate in getting your visitors to contact you. Look to see what's on those pages that may not be on the others. Chances are they have a clearer, more obvious, *call to action* (text and links directing your visitors on what action to take at that point on your site - call, email, come in, etc.).

Your tracking software can also tell you which browsers your visitors are using (Internet Explorer, Firefox, Safari, Chrome, etc.). If you start to see that you're getting a lot of visitors using mobile phones or tablets computers to view your website, that's your hint to start considering a mobile version of your site. Before you design the mobile site for them, ask your visitors what they're looking to do on those mobile devices when they get to your site. Their needs on the go are likely to be different than their needs at home or in their office. This will help you design a mobile site that gives them exactly what they want, without overloading it with unnecessary content.

Identifying Peak Traffic Periods

Look at the times of day and days of the week during which your site is busiest. TheKnot.com—the busiest of all wedding sites—is busiest during the week, during the day... while their target audience is at work. It's no wonder more brides are e-mailing wedding vendors rather than calling: They can't call, or their bosses will bust them for planning their weddings on company time. They can, however, e-mail wedding vendors without getting caught.

This is going to be true of many businesses and industries. If you're selling primarily to a consumer audience, as opposed to business-to-business, and you see that your site is busiest during work hours, don't expect a lot of phone calls during the day. Your prospects probably can't make personal phone calls from work. Check your phone logs as well. Are people calling after your normal business hours? If so, it might be time to reevaluate your "normal" business hours, or invest in a call center or answering service.

Why else do you want to know the busiest days and times for your website? If you're targeting consumers, and you see that most of your traffic is coming in while your prospects are at work, consider removing music or video with sound from your home page that starts to play automatically. The quickest way for visitors to make your music stop is not by clicking that subtle on/off switch; it's by closing their web browser or hitting the BACK button. Unless you're in the music or video business, you probably don't need audio or video on your site at all. If you do have audio or video samples, give your visitors the option to listen or watch—don't start the sound automatically. That way, your visitors can choose to revisit your site outside of work hours or with headphones on.

Keyword Optimization

Next, look at your site's tracking software to see which keywords people are using when they "find" your site on search engines. Look at the bounce rate for the visitors who come to your site using different keyword searches. The lower the bounce rate for a set of keywords, the more relevant your site is for that particular keyword or phrase. This means that the people who come to your site using that set of keywords are more promising as potential customers. There's no magic bounce rate that you're aiming for, just know that lower is almost always better.

Remember, not all clicks are created equal, so even a particular set of keywords with a high bounce rate could still be providing a very profitable return for your business. You have to connect the dots and see how much revenue those clicks are bringing in. If few of the people who are coming from those searches are sticking around but they're making big purchases, then you can certainly live with a high bounce rate. Revenue per click is they key figure.

The Limitations of Tracking Software

If you're a service business, which most of you reading this are, your website tracking software can't tell you if your ads are bringing you any business. Your sales happen offline. The reports can tell you the number of people who click on a particular link, the total number of visitors, the bounce rate, the number of pages viewed, how visitors move around within your site from page to page and much more. The problem here is that unless you understand how to read the reports from your tracking software and then connect the dots to the offline sales, you're making decisions based upon incomplete information. Your car's speedometer tells you how fast you're going, but not what the speed limit is. The tachometer tells you how fast your engine is turning, but not which gear your car is in or in which direction you're headed. Similarly, you need to gather more information from additional sources to make the right decisions for marketing your business and designing your website. Again, consider asking the people who contact you how they got to your website, how they heard about your business and where they got your email or phone number. This will help you determine the conversion rate for each form of advertising and search keyword.

Knowing how much business you book and your ROI from each source of traffic (e.g., advertising on Google or TheKnot.com) will help you make better decisions on where to invest your marketing dollars.

A couple of notes about advertising: While your ROI will likely be different from each source of traffic, you'll want to make sure you're consistent in your marketing investment, during both good times and bad. Don't create your own personal recession by cutting back your marketing when times are good. That's likely what got you busy in the first place. Don't turn off the flow. Some of the most successful businesses ramp up their marketing when they hear others are cutting back. It's the perfect time to increase their market share.

Don't shy away from a particular advertising vehicle because of the number of other advertisers. If the audience is large enough then there should be plenty of prospects to go around. It makes sense that the magazine with the best readership, or the website with the most visitors, would have the most ads just as it makes sense that more fisherman would want to fish in the lake with the most fish. As long as there are enough of the right prospects to go around, the number of ads is likely a sign that there's a desirable audience there too.

CHAPTER SEVEN

Why Now?

Did you ever stop to think about why someone visits your website and then contacts you for more information on a particular day and time? I mean, why now? Why not yesterday? Why not tomorrow? Welcome to my world, because this is the kind of stuff I think about. Was it your print advertising? Was it a search engine? Was it an online ad or a link from another website? It's rarely one thing, but there's almost always a trigger that gets a visitor to your site and then to contact you on a particular day and time. This is one of those moments when you need to sit back and think, *"Yeah, why did they go to my site and e-mail me today of all days?"*

Chances are, they're in that stage of the buying cycle, so they're ripe for the picking when something triggers them to take action. Just make sure you're on a tree in the orchard in which they're looking. You don't want to be the best piece of fruit in an orchard that few people visit. That means ensuring that the advertising methods you're using are reaching a large number of people in your target audience.

Identifying the Action Triggers

Knowing what the action triggers are will also help your marketing. If you can find a way to *trigger* them to visit your site and then to make that initial contact, you'll be able to convert more of the right people into new customers. That will give you more control over the business you book. Make sure there are clear, relevant, calls to action on every page of your website. Don't assume your prospects will know or be moved to take action without them.

CHAPTER EIGHT

You Don't Get a Second Chance to Make a First Impression

Once a potential client starts looking for a particular service, they'll spend a period of time looking over all of the choices. It may be a short or long period depending upon your industry, product or service. This is an important decision for them, so they'll want to consider all of the options. Make sure you put forward the best first impression, or you may not get a second chance.

Get Your Ad Where It Will Be Seen

As they near the decision point, prospects interacting with a media website will look at many of the ads in a category and whittle their choices down to a smaller group. That's why—just as with real estate—location is key. The ads that a potential client sees *first* often get viewed more frequently than those that are less visible. Being at the top of the list doesn't mean you're the right choice for each client, but it does highly increase your chances of being seen. And obviously, once you've got good placement, ensure that you've got a great ad that will catch the viewer's attention and get them to move that attention on to your website.

Why Should They Choose You?

Do you know the purchasing decision timeline for your product or service? I once read that when someone starts going out looking for a car, they usually buy within 72 hours. That means that a car salesman has to make a very good first impression, or their customer is likely to move on to the next dealership. The customer can buy the exact same car from other dealers, so why should they choose any one in particular? It's likely the same for your business: Prospects can buy your product or service, or something they perceive as similar, at other businesses, so why should they buy from you? That's a question that you'll want to answer right away for your potential clients—whether or not they come right out and ask it.

Lookin' Sharp

Once you get a prospect's attention, you had better put your best foot forward. Use professional, eye-catching photos with beautiful color. For ads, remember: You're trying to catch someone's attention, so make sure you choose the right image for your marketing medium. If the first photo a prospect sees is a small, thumbnail sized photo—as it is on many online ads and all mobile ads—then choose a photo that actually looks good at that size. You may have a signature image that looks great in a full page print ad or on the wall of your office, but does it look good at the size of a postage stamp? Does it stand out among the other postage stamp sized images? Will someone who's never seen it know what it is immediately?

Why am I asking you so many questions? Because only you can find the best answers for your business. My role is to help you find those answers by asking you the right questions. I'm just guiding you down the road you've already chosen: the road that leads to better website design and more effective advertising.

CHAPTER NINE

Question 3: What Do Your Customers Want to See and Do on Your Website?

Now you know who your target audience is and that the first place they're likely to go after they hear about you is to your website. But what do they want to see and do once they get there?

Think back to our discussion of how they got to your site in the first place. Where they came from tells you a little about what—if anything—they already know about you. It will also give you a clue as to what they're expecting to find on your site. This is another one of those times when your website tracking software can help you. If you see that visitors are using certain search terms, those terms will tell you what your prospects are looking for when they visit your site.

What Media Are They Using to Visit Your Site?

Again, what if your tracking software shows you that visitors are using a mobile device to access your site? Think about what it is they want to see on their mobile device. As we previously discussed, find out from your site visitors exactly what it is they're trying to access on your site with their mobile devices. Their needs on the go usually very different than they are at work or at home. This will help you design a mobile site that gives them the most value, and therefore the most connection, to your site. You'll likely find that much of the content on your main website doesn't translate well to the small size of the screen on a mobile device.

Continue the Conversation

If your tracking software shows that visitors are coming from a particular online ad, then you want to continue the "conversation" that you started on the ad, and that attracted them in the first place. If they're coming in from an e-mail campaign or direct mailing, again, try to continue the conversation that was started in the e-mail or postcard. Did you make a special offer? Does the page on which they "land" repeat the offer? If not, there's a disconnect between the e-mail or postcard and your site. You need to confirm for visitors that they've landed at the right place by ensuring that the branding, colors and design for your site match your marketing materials, and they repeat the message and offer contained in those materials. Then, add more value and a strong call to action to help your conversion rate.

Too often, I see businesses doing e-mail or direct mail campaigns without making any changes on their sites or creating a landing page. They just direct the prospects to their home page, and then wonder why few people who contact them ever mention the offer. It's likely because the people who see the marketing material and then visit the site don't feel a connection with the marketing material that led them to there—and so they never become customers. If they go to the trouble of visiting your site after seeing your e-mail or direct mail campaigns, they're obviously interested in your company. So turn that interest into a sale by giving them more of what got them to your site in the first place. You'll likely see an increased ROI if you think of your site as an *extension* of the e-mail or direct mail campaign. Again, just *continue* the conversation from where your marketing material left off.

And Surveys Say...

The best way to know what your customers want to see and do on your site is simply to ask them. Survey your current and past customers and ask them what it is they'd like to see and do on your website. Be as specific as possible with your questions, and keep them open ended so you don't influence people's answers. Try not to ask "Yes" or "No" questions, as they provide you with very little information. Instead of asking, "Do you want to see photo galleries?", ask, *"How many photos would you like to see in our online photo gallery?", "What types of photos would you like to see in our photo gallery?" or even "How would you like the photos to be organized?"*

CHAPTER TEN

Question 4: What Do You Want Your Customers to See and Do on Your Website?

What do you want your prospects to see and do when they get to your site? What's your end goal?

Service Businesses

Most of you reading this likely run or work for a service business. And if that's the case, prospects can't enter their credit card information and make a purchase on your site, so making a sale is *not* your end goal. They have to meet with—or at least speak with *you* - for you to be able to make that sale. **For service businesses, the end goal for your site is getting visitors to contact you so that you can make that sale.** Own or accept that so you can refocus on the right goal.

Product Businesses

If, on the other hand, your main business is to sell products directly through your website, then your end goal is to get prospects to complete the purchase process online. You want them to put items into their carts and complete the checkout process without abandoning their carts. I recently read that the average abandon rate for online shopping carts is 40 percent. Site visitors find an item that interests them, and they put the item into their shopping carts... but they leave the site without completing their purchase. Why? Sometimes it's because the checkout process is too cumbersome, too intrusive or intimidating, or just too slow.

Where Are You Losing Your Visitors?

Here again is another place that your tracking software is very helpful: Product-based businesses need to identify where prospects are bailing out from their sites. Which page is the last your prospects visited? At what stage in the checkout process did they abandon their intended purchases? Or, did they leave without putting anything in their carts at all?

This goes for service businesses as well. Obviously you won't have a shopping cart, but from which pages are prospects leaving your site? And how many pages have they seen before they leave? As we've discussed, if they've only seen one page, they've bounced from your site. What if they're viewing five pages and then leaving without contacting you?

Once you know where they decide to leave your site, look for ways to keep them on your site or to encourage them see more pages and to contact you. Sometimes all you need is a clearer call to action and easy navigation paths. Maybe—just maybe—they're leaving because you're not asking them to stay, or you're not giving them a good reason to stay, or you're not giving them what they want to see.

With this valuable information from your tracking software, you can improve your menus, navigation, calls to action and content to help direct visitors to the things you most want them to see and do. Find the weakest areas and either remove or improve them.

The Value of Good Content

And this leads us to the next question: Can you defend the content on your site? Why is it there and how does it help move your visitors closer to becoming customers? That content may be important to you, but you need to find out if it's important to your target audience. Before you just start loading something up on your site, ask yourself if prospects would, or should, care about it. If it's something they should care about, then make sure that you present it in such a way that they understand not only what it is, but *why* it should be important to them. This is a really critical point. You need to get your prospects to understand not only what you're trying to tell them, but also how that information will help them achieve *their* ultimate goal—be it having the perfect wedding, having beautiful photos to help them immortalize their special day, or whatever service it is you're providing them —by doing business with you.

And don't assume that just because one of your competitors has something on their site it means their customers want to see it or are even looking at those pages. Don't design your site to impress your industry friends. They're not your target audience. Putting something on your site doesn't guarantee anyone will see it or that they'll care.

Satisfying Your Needs and the Needs of Your Clients

The goal is to match up what prospects want to see and do with what you want them to see and do as seamlessly as possible. That's why having relevant calls to action on every page—even more than once on a page—is so critical. So let's talk about your site's calls to action.

Frequent Calls to Action

As you just read, every page on your site should have a call to action, although the wording can change from page to page. For instance, a photo gallery page on a wedding photographer's or planner's site could say, *"To see more beautiful photos like these, call Debbie today to arrange an appointment: 800-555-1234."* The testimonial page on almost any site could say, *"Call today to find out how you can become our next satisfied customer: 800-555-1234."*

Treat each page's calls to action as a separate invitation: Think about what the visitor is doing on that page, and what action you want them to take next. You don't know what page they'll be on when they decide to contact you, so assume that it can be any page on your site. Redundancy is good when it comes to your calls to action and contact information.

CHAPTER ELEVEN

Are You Talking to Me?

Talk to Your Audience About Them, Not About You

The easiest way to do this is to make sure you're using the words "you" and "your" more than you use "I," "we," "me," "us" or "our." Write as if you're speaking to your prospects in person so they feel your personality coming through. Addressing your words directly to your visitors will make them feel more connected to your content, and ultimately to you. This is one of those easy things you can do to improve your current site, even if you have a brand new site in the works. If you tackle this one page at a time, not the whole site at once, you'll get this done quickly.

Clearly Tell Your Visitors Their Next Step

Give prospects a reason to want more information. Then tell them what you want them to do and make it easy for them to do it. If you want them to call you, tell them to *call,* tell them *why they're calling* (for an appointment, brochure, sample DVD, price, etc.) and then give them your phone number, no matter how many times it already appears on that page or your site. Don't make them click again to see your phone number.

If you want your prospects to e-mail you, it works the same way. Clearly tell them to e-mail you, why they're e-mailing (for an appointment, brochure, sample DVD, price, etc.) and then follow those words with a link to your e-mail address or contact form. If you use an e-mail contact form, consider adding the question, *"How did you find our website today?"* By the time you get to meet with the prospect, they're usually too far removed from the original source to give you an accurate answer to this question.

Make It Personal

If you can personalize the contact request by telling the prospect who they're calling or e-mailing, your invitation to connect will seem friendlier and more conversational. If the prospect then calls and asks for "Stacy," this will feel much more personal than their asking for *"someone* to talk to about a wedding." Then, when the prospect gets an e-mail reply from "Stacy," it will be confirmation that a real person is taking interest in them.

CHAPTER TWELVE

The Curse of Knowledge

A concept that comes up over and over again in my work, my personal life and my presentations is the idea that once you know something, it's very hard to go about the task at hand as if you didn't know it. This is called the Curse of Knowledge, and it's a subject that's been written about many, many times.

But What's Your Address?

So how does this affect your business? I've seen websites with no address listed, yet they're for retail stores. On a recent trip, my wife and I were looking for a natural foods store in Rhode Island. We used my iPad to do a Google search, and it came up with one in the next town from where we were at the time. I clicked through to the store's site, and it wasn't bad, just a little dated. The pages loaded quickly and listed many of the brands and products that they carried... but where were they located? I searched around the site for their address. It wasn't on their home page. It wasn't on their contact page (this was just an e-mail form, which I can't stand, by the way: When prospects click on your contact page, they should see ALL of the ways to contact you, not just an e-mail form. I can hear your heads nodding in agreement.). I looked at about five pages until I finally found their location on the "About Us" page.

This was a retail store, on a main street: Isn't it a given that a store would have its address on the home page, if not on *every* page? I would think so, but when I mentioned to the checkout clerk at the store that their address wasn't on their home page, she seemed surprised. She had been to their site many times, but she had never noticed that the address wasn't listed prominently. Why? She already knew the store's address, so she wasn't looking for it. She wasn't thinking like a new customer. In fact, it would be very difficult for her to think like a new customer because she has the Curse of Knowledge.

How Can They Call You If They Don't Have Your Phone Number?

I realize that these days, when you're dealing with a younger audience, they're becoming less and less likely to pick up the phone and call you (as opposed to e-mailing), but that doesn't mean you should take your phone number off your site altogether. Some prospects will want to call you before the sale, while others will want to call after e-mailing or booking you. If you're targeting a wedding audience, very often the bride's mother is helping with the research. Mom is more likely to want to call you than her daughter. Not providing your phone number is ludicrous from a marketing standpoint. What that says to *me* is that you're not that comfortable with the sales process. A professional sales person's primary goal for marketing is almost always to get a phone call from their prospects. A call is the most effective way to get an appointment and, subsequently, the sale. And don't you want to make the sale?

I've also seen too many websites provide a phone number without the area code. Prospects outside your area may not know what your area code is. With the increasing number of people using cell phones, there are new area codes popping up every year. It costs you nothing to add those three digits, so just do it. If you only list a toll free phone number and no address, thinking you're casting a wider net, you could be losing local customers who don't see you as local.

Don't Let Your Curse of Knowledge Hurt Your Website

Ask yourself how the Curse of Knowledge is affecting what you put on your website. Are you using any abbreviations or acronyms that are common knowledge to you and your industry friends, but not so common to your target audience? For example, a hotel may say, *"Submit an RFP"* on its wedding page, but that's corporate language meaning "request for proposal," not necessarily the language a bride would know or use. Are you assuming that your target audience knows more about you, or your industry, than they actually do? Are you assuming that you know what's important to them instead of asking them what they think is important? It's hard to put yourself in your prospects' shoes, but the better you can learn to do that, the better your return will be.

CHAPTER THIRTEEN

Referrals Are Your Biggest Source of New Business... or Are They?

I know that many businesses think referrals are the top reason that someone does business with them, but in this crowded and noisy marketing world in which we live, it's just not that simple.

In fact, we're all being influenced every day by media, personal experience and, of course, word of mouth. Each of these holds some sway over our decisions, and some influence us more than others. For example, we view different media sources with varying levels of trust. We trust the referrals from some people more than we do from others. Therefore, if we get multiple referrals, all pointing us to a different company, each referral does not carry the same weight. This is influenced by who has given the referrals as well as the way they've given the referrals.

How Is the Referral Delivered, and Who's Giving It?

Let's say you ask a neighbor to refer a good plumber. Your neighbor says, *"I use Acme Plumbing."* Then you ask a different neighbor the same question, and they say, *"I love Matt's Plumbing because they're very clean, they show up on time and they always come in at, or under, the price they quoted."* These are both referrals, but which one is stronger? That's an easy one. The referrer who provides specific examples of why they use a particular plumber (i.e., the plumber is *clean, timely* and there are no surprise costs) is more persuasive than the referrer who gives no information about why they use their plumber.

Have you ever stopped to think about this in terms of your business? Some of the people referred to you are getting information like the first example and some like the second. What's more, you must also take into account who the referral came from: A referral from an acquaintance at work is not the same as one that a prospect receives from their sister or best friend.

Consider the Whole Picture

Now, let's take things further and look at this in terms of the connected world in which we live. So, add to the referrals that people make for your business the advertising you do and online reviews. If a consumer who was referred to you has an affinity and trust for the magazine, website or trade show where you advertise, they will automatically have a more favorable view of your company. Even if the prospect didn't see your ad, but makes it to your website where they see the phrase, *"As seen on TheKnot.com"* (or whatever media you use for ads), this will support or even raise the prospect's impression of your business. Throw in some positive comments on a message board or reviews engine, maybe a testimonial or two, and each of these helps drive that referred prospect even closer to you.

So Is There a Problem Here?

Not really, unless you're trying to closely track your advertising and marketing. If you wait until you meet with that customer to ask them how they found you, they're usually too far removed from the advertising to be able to honestly indicate if it played a part in their decision. So if you ask them, *"How did you hear about us?"*, they'll likely answer with the name of the person who first told them about your company, even though all of those other exposures—ads, message boards and reviews—also influenced their decision to contact you.

This can, and does, go the other way as well, only you'll never get to talk to those people since they were influenced *away* from you. You also don't get to talk to the people who have gotten stronger signals and influence that moved them toward another business. Just keep this in mind: **Prospects trust the message (i.e., referral) more when they trust the messenger, so align yourself with the right messengers and don't take referrals for granted: nurture them.**

CHAPTER FOURTEEN

What Information Should You Have on Your Site and How Should You Display It?

Once you've determined what your site visitors want to do and what you want them to do, you need to decide what information should be on your site and how to display it.

What Pages Should Your Site Have?

You can't just list everything on one page... or can you? If your business is very easy to explain, and it doesn't need a lot of photos or other information, then maybe you can just have one web page. Don't feel that your site has to have a certain number or type of pages just because other sites do. There's no magic number of pages for a website. Too much information (TMI) usually is not better.

For example, if you perform wedding ceremonies, you may be able to have just one, well designed page. It could showcase a couple of nice, professional photos of you performing ceremonies; some concise, descriptive text explaining what you do; perhaps your rates; and a strong call to action. If you feel you need more than that, then you can always add pages later. However, be careful not to get carried away by making your one page so long that visitors have to scroll down continually. Personally, if I see a site where I have to click "page down" more than once, I've lost interest already, and I'm sure you have too.

If you do have a contact page, make sure that it's complete. As we've discussed previously, when prospects click on your contact page, they should see ALL of the ways to contact you, not just an e-mail form. In addition to your contact form, they should see your address (if it's pertinent to your business), easy directions, including landmarks and a map, your phone number(s) and your hours of operation. Put yourself in the shoes of your prospects. What would you want to find there if you were the customer? Similarly, if you see something you don't like on a site you visit... don't do that on your own site.

Side Note About Writing for the Benefit of SEO

If you work from home and don't want your street address listed, that's okay. Just remember that if you don't list any location information on your site, in real text (not a graphic or Flash) then the search engines don't know where your business is based. Local searches is one of the fastest growing categories so be sure you're in the game. Search engines "index" your site by reading the text on pages on your site. This tells them who you are, what you do and where you're located. They take this information and use it to return the most relevant search results when their users perform a search using some of the words that appear on a page on your site. So, even if you don't list your full address, be sure to provide your business's general location. You can also do this by using captions on the photos on your site identifying their location and in your blog posts, writing about the places where you do business and where your customers are coming from. These help to localize you even when you don't list your physical address.

Using Menus Effectively

For the most part, visitors prefer websites whose information is organized into clearly labeled menu items so they can easily choose what to see and do.

Then, those menu items should lead to pages with well-organized, concise content. The beautiful thing here is that you get to decide what your site's menu items are, so *you* decide what choices your visitors have. Be sure to label the menus clearly. I see too many websites that use non-standard menu titles just for the sake of being different. It's much more important to label your menus in such a way that visitors can easily find what they're looking for. If a prospect doesn't know what they're going to find when they click on a menu item, they often won't bother to click at all. Use the language that they use so your menus appear more intuitive to them.

I remember a photographer telling me that his rates were on his website, yet brides were calling and asking for his prices (which to me was a good thing-They were calling him). Just because something is on your site doesn't mean anyone is seeing it. Again, make sure that the items your prospects will think are most important are clearly labeled and easy to locate.

If you want to draw your prospects' attention to a non-menu item, you can also use links to get them where you want them to go. However, a text link can very easily get visually overshadowed by graphical elements on that same page. Don't underline any text that's not a link as it will confuse your prospects. Your visitor's attention is going to the things that jump out and scream, "Look at me!" and a text link doesn't usually do that. There are many tasteful ways to direct your visitors to the things you most want them to see and do. A good website designer can help you identify the best ways to do this. However, if you meet with your website designer by looking in the mirror, it's up to you to poll your customers, and potential customers, to see how they perceive your site and it's content. Then, use that information to rework your site to improve your conversion.

CHAPTER FIFTEEN

Question 5: How Often Will They, or Should They, Return to Your Site?

We've arrived at question number five: How often will—or should—your prospects return to your site? Will they see enough on their first visit to make them take action, or will they have to come back? Will they even want to come back? What are their needs on each visit? I can hear you saying, *"Alan, why are you asking me so many questions? Can't you just give me the answers?"* Well, I wish I could, but the magic wand store was closed, and their website was terrible—so I abandoned my shopping cart.

How Long Is the Buying Process for Your Prospects?

You have to understand your consumer. Do they buy soon after they start looking, or is there a longer research phase? For instance, brides spend about three months searching for the perfect wedding gown before they make a purchase. As I've mentioned before, car buyers tend to buy within about three days of when they begin visiting dealerships. How long is the buying process of your best prospects—the ones who eventually make a purchase with you?

When it comes to your prospective clients, design your site for the second and third time they visit, not just the first. You don't navigate through a website the same way the second or third time as you do on the first visit, so don't expect that your prospects will either. What path will they take through your site the first time, the second time, or even after you make the sale? Are those different paths clear? Remember earlier when I said that you control the choices your prospects have because you control the links and menu items? It's up to you to only give them the choices that are necessary. Really ask yourself about the content, links and menus on your site. Why are they there, and how do they help your visitors get closer to their goal, and yours?

If your site can track whether someone is a first time or repeat visitor, it will help you understand the buying process and flow of your site. If you can take it one step further and see which pages they view on the first visit versus subsequent visits, it will help you decide if your menus, text, images and links are directing them to what you want them to see. If you can get your visitors to "sign in," then you can closely follow them through your site to see how they interact with it.

Should You Serve Different Content to Prospects and Customers?

Some websites have separate areas for prospects and customers. These different areas may include forms or documents that site visitors will need at different stages: before, during and after the sale is made. Some business owners, like photographers, have public photo galleries for their prospects, and password-protected galleries for their current customers. The current customers, as well as their friends and family, can access these "gated" areas to see, and buy, photos and prints.

Will *your* customers want or need to come back after they make a purchase? If so, what is it that they'll want to see and do after the sale? Are their needs after the sale so different from their needs before the sale that you need to consider building a separate website for them? Would a different landing page for customers than prospects make them feel more welcomed? Would it show them that you understand that their needs are different now and that you care about fulfilling their current needs? In many cases I would think so.

One thing that may help you decide whether or not you need separate sites or hidden areas is that you don't want to alienate your prospects by locking up too much content. If you have different sites, or addresses, for post-sale clients, you won't frustrate your pre-sale prospects by showing them a link, and then denying them access because that area is "gated" (password protected). No one likes hitting a dead end. Later, after they make a purchase, you can e-mail them a link to "their" area with the relevant content for them in their new role as customer, rather than prospect.

Plan for the Future

Do you have up-sell opportunities to current customers when they come back to your site? If yes, then knowing that the visitor is a returning customer is very important so that you can suggest other opportunities for them. Again, try to find out how many visits they'll make, and at what point in the sales process they are, so that you can understand their needs during each visit.

CHAPTER SIXTEEN

There Is No Change without Action

How do you feel now? You've gotten through all five things you wish you knew before you made your website. Will you complete the title and fix them now? The definition of *futility* (or *insanity,* if you prefer) is doing the same thing, the same way, and expecting a different result. In order to benefit from what you've just learned, you have to decide to take some action.

Don't worry: You don't need to tackle all of this at once. There are easy wins on every website: small changes that you can make, or have made, will have an impact. Making many small changes will ultimately add up to big results.

If you've determined that you need a new—or additional—website, what can you do in the meantime to your existing site? Can you tweak some of the wording to be more customer-centric (remember: use "you" and "your" more than "I," "we," "us", and "me")? Can you add a relevant call to action on every page? Can you link your advertising and marketing to the most appropriate page on your site? Of course you can. These are easy fixes.

I'm going to leave you with a great piece of advice that I got at one of the first National Speakers Association meetings I ever attended: Make a list of all the great ideas you now have for your website, and then prioritize the list in terms of how much impact each item will have on your business, and how quickly you can implement it. If something is a fairly big project (like making an entirely new website), then break it up into smaller pieces (such as researching website design companies, finding domain names, mapping out which content belongs on that site, etc.) and consider each one a separate task.

Once you have the big list of all of your great ideas, keep the top three things on the list, and then get rid of the rest. You'll be more likely to take action this way. Larger projects that can be broken down into smaller pieces will often appear on your list, so it may take a while to get through all the pieces of a large project but you'll be making progress instead of just thinking about what you're going to do.

When you complete the three things on your list, make a new list. It's very likely that number four on your original list will not be number one on your new list. It may not even be on your list at all now. After you complete each list of three items, just make a new one. It will feel much more satisfying to cross off one of three items on your list, rather than one of thirty. There's a greater sense of accomplishment and it will motivate you to tackle the other two items on your list.

So, now that we're at the end of the road, I hope you've thought of some things you can do to improve your site. Have you started your list yet? What action are you going to take... today? You know that your website is the most likely first stop for your prospects and customers. They may not even have the opportunity to talk to you or meet with you if your website isn't doing its job.

Ask yourself this: If your website was an employee, would you retrain it, fire it or give it a raise? It's all up to you now.

Thanks for spending this time with me and best of luck.

THE MOVEMENT OF
WORLD REVOLUTION